Cover illustration: The M109 International Turret programme is a joint venture between Royal Ordnance in Britain and BMY in the United States. It is intended as a product improvement for the many M109s outside the USA or as a new production version in lieu of the US M109 HIP. It is also called the M109TX. (BMY)

1. The M109 is crewed by ten men, six of whom can be carried on board while it is travelling. It carries up to 28 rounds of conventional ammunition. These two vehicles belonged to Battery 'C', 1st Howitzer Battalion, 94th Artillery, 4th Armored Division, and are seen at the Grafenwohr Training Area in the Federal Republic of Germany, 7 March 1964. The M109 entered production in 1961 and entered service use in 1962. (US Army)

TANKS ILLUSTRATED No 26

US MECHANIZED FIREPOWER TODAY

STEVEN J. ZALOGA &
ARNOLD MEISNER

ARMS AND ARMOUR PRESS
London New York Sydney

Introduction

First published in Great Britain in 1987 by Arms and Armour Press Ltd., Artillery House, Artillery Row, London SW1P 1RT.

Distributed in the USA by Sterling Publishing Co. Inc., 2 Park Avenue, New York, NY 10016.

Distributed in Australia by Capricorn Link (Australia) Pty. Ltd., P.O. Box 665, Lane Cove, New South Wales 2066, Australia.

British Library Cataloguing in Publication Data:
Zaloga, Steven J.
U.S. mechanized firepower today. – (Tanks illustrated; v.26)
1. United States. *Army*. 2. Tanks (Military science) – United States
I. Title II. Meisner, Arnold III. Series
623.74′752′0973 UG446.5

ISBN 0-85368-732-3

Edited and designed by Roger Chesneau; typeset by Typesetters (Birmingham) Ltd.; printed and bound in Great Britain by The Bath Press, Avon.

◀2
2. The M60 AVLB is a scissors bridge system. The bridge is hydraulically lifted, and then opened up, scissors fashion, across the gap. The tracked transporter can recover it from either side. (Pierre Touzin)

Tanks and armoured infantry vehicles are probably the best known of modern AFVs, but beyond these is a bewildering array of other equipment used to defend tanks from air attack, to provide fire support for tank and infantry attacks, to support engineer operations and to recover and repair other armoured vehicles. The aim of this volume is to show the wide range of vehicles designed for these many roles and currently in use with, or being developed by, the US Army.

The self-propelled artillery of the US Army has changed little in the past two decades, the M109 155mm and M110 8in self-propelled howitzers, developed in the late 1950s, having proved to be effective, reliable weapons, and field artillery modernization programmes have been aimed at improving these basic systems and their ammunition and fire control equipment. With the advent of laser-guided anti-tank artillery projectiles like the 155mm M712 Copperhead, however, the need arose for a fire support team designation and targeting vehicle, which entered service in 1985 as the M981 FIST. US Army studies concluded that the main limitation in fire support was not so much a shortage of guns but inadequate availability of ammunition on the battlefield, and as a result the M992 FAASV was developed to replace trucks in supplying self-propelled artillery with ammunition. The US Army is the first to adopt this type of vehicle in significant numbers. New versions of the M109 and M110 continue to appear, and replacements for these systems are unlikely to appear for at least another decade. The most novel vehicle on the US field artillery inventory is the new M270 MLRS multiple rocket launcher.

The situation with US Army air defence is far more complicated and chaotic. In the 1960s the very sophisticated and ambitious Mauler air defence missile and Vigilante air defence gun programmes failed as a result of technical shortcomings and high costs. The M163 VADS air defence gun vehicle and M48 Chaparral air defence missile vehicle were adopted as interim solutions, but the US Army had hoped to replace these with, respectively, the M247 Sergeant York DIVAD and XM975 Roland. The Roland was a victim of its high costs, and only a handful were ever fielded, whilst the DIVAD programme suffered from high costs, technical problems and a changing threat – by the mid-1980s Soviet helicopters firing anti-tank missiles from long, stand-off ranges had become a greater threat than jet attack aircraft and, unfortunately, DIVAD was not entirely capable of adapting to this new problem. As a result, the US Army is still saddled with the completely inadequate M163A1 VADS. The M48A2 Chaparral has adapted somewhat better to the changing air defence environment, thanks to substantial technological advances in infrared missile seeker technology; however, although Chaparral is very effective against jet attack aircraft it is less suitable for the anti-helicopter role, and the US Army is currently looking for a new system as part of the FAADS programme. Some of the many candidates are illustrated in this book.

There is a wide variety of combat vehicles in service with the US Army, including armoured recovery vehicles like the M88 and M578 and combat engineer vehicles such as the M728 CEV, M60 AVLB and M9 ACE. These play an essential role in modern mechanized warfare by keeping the rest of the Army's vehicles moving.

This book would not have been possible without the generous help of friends who provided many of the photographs used here, and the authors would like especially to thank Pierre Touzin, whose fine studies of US vehicles in Europe considerably enhance this volume. Thanks go also to Leif Hellstrom, Brian Gibbs, Bob Lessels of the PAO/TECOM at Aberdeen Proving Grounds (APG) and Scott Gourley of the FMC Corporation for their kind assistance.
Steven Zaloga and Arnold Meisner

▲3

3. The M109 has been the US Army's standard medium self-propelled 155mm howitzer since 1962. The initial version, seen here, was fitted with the short M126 cannon. This particular vehicle (photographed at Fort Hood, Texas, during an Armed Forces Day exhibition in the early 1970s) belonged to the 1/14th Field Artillery. The regimental crest can be seen in front of the vehicle, and a simplified portion, the circled Maltese cross, can be seen as a unit insignia on the turret front. (Brian Gibbs)

4. The M109A1 introduced the new M185 gun tube in 1972. The tube is 84in longer, and permits longer-range fire for the howitzer. M109s converted to this standard are classified as M109A1, new production vehicles with the new tube being designated M109A1B. This vehicle is one of 390 M109s and M109A1s supplied to Iran prior to the fall of the Shah: it was used in the Gulf War, was captured by Iraq, and is seen here in Baghdad. Many of these captured M109s were used by Iraqi forces, and the olive drab and sand camouflage may be evidence of this since the Iranian vehicles were normally finished in a uniform sand colour. (Leif Hellstrom)

▼4

5▲

5. In 1979, the M109A2 and -A3 were introduced. The M109A3 is an M109A1 upgraded with a PIP (Product Improvement Program) kit to include the improved M178 gun mount, simplified hydraulics and other internal improvements; the M109A2 is a new production vehicle incorporating these features from the outset. It is almost impossible to distinguish between these sub-types except upon very close inspection, and for this reason both types are collectively referred to here as M109A2. It is, however, possible to distinguish the M109A2 from the M109A1 by the rear turret extension and by the ballistic cover over the sighting port; in this view, the rear turret extension is clearly evident. (Pierre Touzin)

6. An M109A2 during the September 1980 'Reforger' exercise in Germany. The enclosed ballistic cover over the panoramic sight can be seen to the right of the M2HB machine gun on the turret roof, and this is the easiest way to tell the M109A2/A3 from the A1. This M109A2 is being reloaded by an M548A1 fully tracked, 6-ton cargo carrier. Each battery of six M109s is usually accompanied by six M548s to carry the remainder of the crew and extra ammunition; the US Army is currently in the process of replacing the unarmoured M548A1 with the armoured M992 FAASV. (Pierre Touzin)

6▼

▲7 ▼8

7. An M109A2 during winter exercises in Germany. It is finished in the four-tone MERDC camouflage pattern – standard on US Army vehicles at the time – but since 1985 the Army has gradually been switching to a NATO three-colour camouflage. (Pierre Touzin)
8. A pair of M109A2s photographed during the August 1982 NATO exercises in Germany. The vehicle to the rear has had its right stowage rack removed, showing more clearly the turret extension added on the M109A2. The long poles on the vehicle sides are probably for the ubiquitous camouflage nets carried by artillery vehicles like these. In 1983 the US Army had about 1,475 M109s, while the US Marine Corps had a further 184; more have been built since then. (Pierre Touzin)
9. A close-up view of the enclosed ballistic sight cover over the panoramic telescope on the M109A2/A3 which distinguishes this model from the earlier M109A1. (S. Zaloga)
10. A rear view of an M109A2 of the 1/3rd Artillery. This is the sixth M109A2 of Battery 'C', evident from the 'C30' bumper code seen on the right mud flap. (S. Zaloga)

9▲

10▼

11. A close-up photograph showing rear detail of the entrenching spades and rear turret stowage on an M109A2. In the field, the stowage bins are used to carry six crew bed-rolls, and the boxes attached to them carry vehicle tools like bore brushes, the gun tool roll and signal markers. (S. Zaloga)
12. An interior view of the left front side of the M109A2 turret; this area is occupied by the gunner (in front) and a loader behind him. The interior is painted gloss white, but the gun breech is gloss black. At the top centre of the photograph is the panoramic sight; lower down can be seen the tunnel which leads to the driver's station, and the right of the picture is filled with the gun breech and power rammer. (S. Zaloga)
13. A view of the right front side of an M109A2. This station is occupied by the assistant gunner and a loader behind him. The gun breech is evident to the left of the photo; in the centre is the M15 elevation quadrant and M118C direct-fire telescope. The large bottle in the centre is the weapon accumulator. (S. Zaloga)
14. A view to the left rear of the M109A2 turret. In the centre are stowage racks for 22 projectiles; the remainder are stowed elsewhere in the fighting compartment. (S. Zaloga)
◀**11**

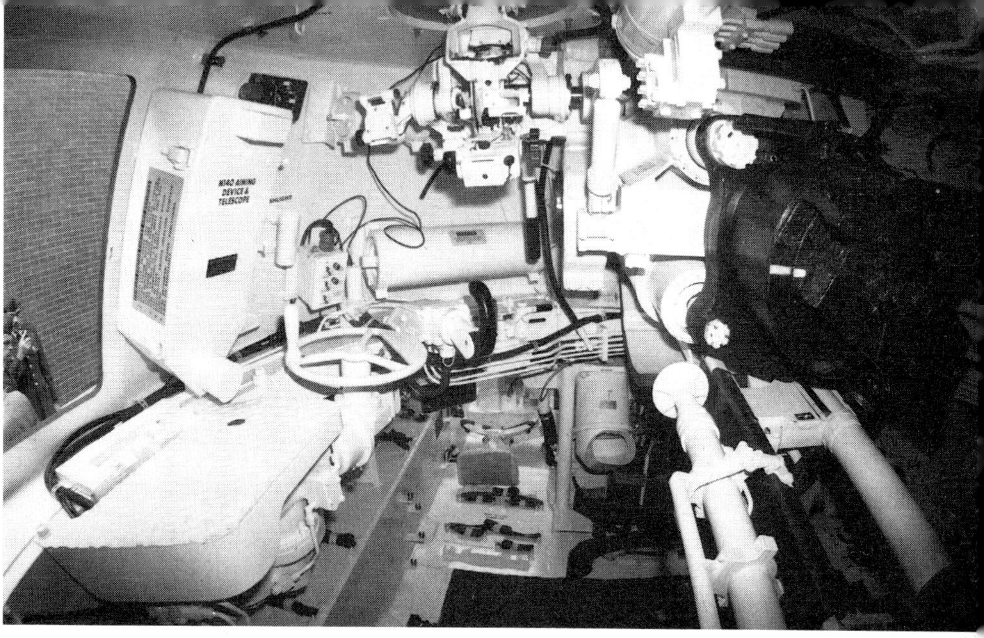

12▲

13▲ **14**▼

15. The M109E4 is one of the prototypes of the HELP (Howitzer Extended Life Program), which will result in the M109A4. The modifications are mainly internal and are connected to efforts to increase the maintainability of the vehicle and improve its fire control. The external alterations include the change in the rear boxes to provide more covered stowage and the provision of larger, open stowage bins on the turret front. This particular prototype was used in experiments to add additional right hull side vents for engine cooling, but this idea was abandoned and the port plated over, as seen here. (S. Zaloga)

16. A bird's-eye view of the M109E4 HELP, clearly showing the new turret stowage bins, which are patterned after similar Israeli bins added to the Zahal's M109A1s. Note also the new gun travel lock on the vehicle bow. (US Army APG)

▲15 ▼16

17▲

17. Another view of one of the M109E4 HELP prototypes, in this case the M109E4-2. This photograph shows the reinforced travel lock and the front turret stowage bins. (US Army APG)

18. An M108 modified for the M109E4 HELP programme, with additional engine cooling vents on the right side of the hull. The M108 was a relative of the M109, mounting a 105mm howitzer. Its career in the US Army was short-lived and the vehicles were subsequently either converted to M109s or used for experimental purposes, as in this case. (US Army APG)

◀**18**

▲19

19. A front view of the current (1986) configuration of the M109E4, showing the travel lock in use. (S. Zaloga)
20. Beyond the M109E4, the US Army is planning a more heavily modified version, the M109A5 HIP (Howitzer Improvement Program), which will incorporate a new gun tube and many fire control and loading improvements. Three teams developed competitive versions of the M109A5 HIP, this one being the Norden/UTC entry which included contributions from FMC Northern Ordnance, AAI, Elbit and Rheinmetall. However, this team, and another headed by General Electric, lost to a consortium headed by BMY, the current manufacturer of the M109, in 1985. When completed, the M109A5 modification programme will eventually encompass about 1,700 US M109s and 600 Israeli vehicles. (S. Zaloga)
21. An overhead view of the turret of the Norden M109A5 HIP prototype, showing the heavy reconfiguration of the turret rear. This modification was necessary to permit the incorporation of a new loading system. (S. Zaloga)
22. A view of the interior of the Norden M109A5 HIP prototype, showing the new gun breech, semi-automatic loader rammer and reconfigured stowage. (S. Zaloga)

▼20

21▲ 22▼

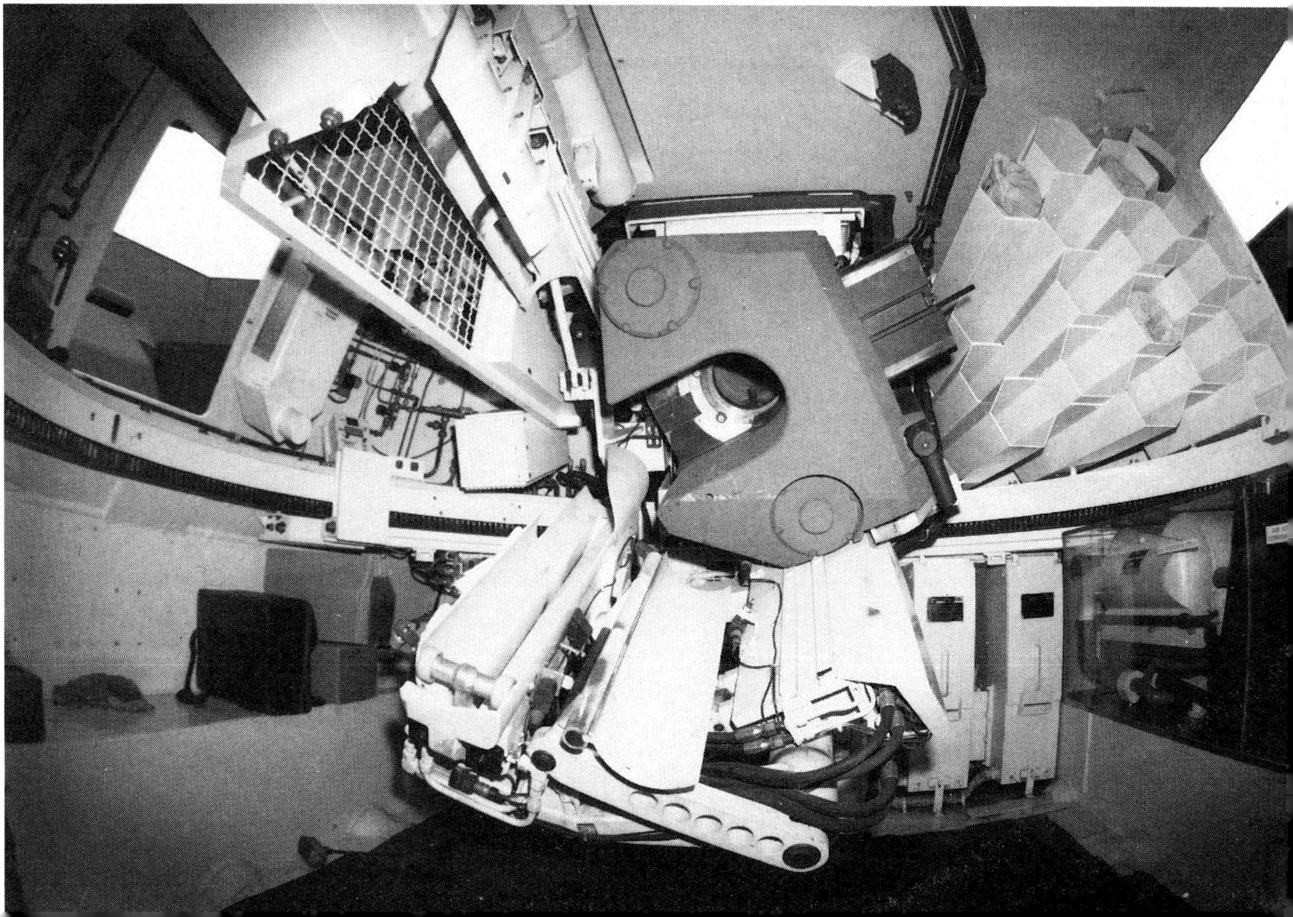

▲23

23. A joint US/British venture for M109 modernization outside United States, the International Turret permits various packages of upgrades to be installed, including a different howitzer and loading features.

24. FMC Northern Ordnance presented this model to show its concept for an M109 Maxi-PIP, which would include an automatic projectile loading system.

25. One of the more unusual versions of the M109 to have appeared in recent years is this 122mm D-30M self-propelled howitzer prototype built for Egypt, which currently manufactures the Soviet 122mm D-30M howitzer and wanted a self-propelled counterpart. This BMY prototype is competing against a British Royal Ordnance entry. Unlike the standard M109, it does not employ a traversing turret. (Christopher Foss)

26. The heavy counterpart to the M109 is the M110 8in (203mm) self-propelled howitzer. The original version of this vehicle appeared in 1963 with the short M2A1E1 cannon on the M158 mount. This particular vehicle is an M110 of the Imperial Iranian Army, which received 38 of them during the Shah's reign. (US Army)

▼24

25▲ 26▼

▲ 28 ▼ 29

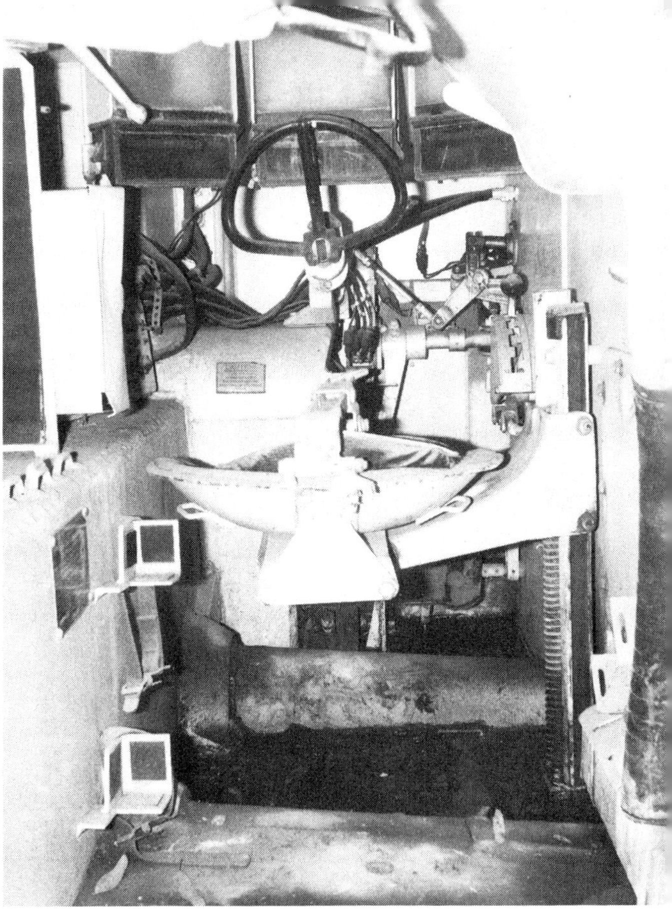

30▲

27. (Previous spread) The M110 was used by both the US Army and the US Marine Corps. Here, two self-propelled howitzers provide fire support for the 4th Marine Amphibious Brigade during exercises in central Norway in September 1976. (USMC)
28. The M110 had a long-ranged counterpart, the M107 175mm self-propelled gun. The M110 andM107 were identical vehicles with interchangeable barrels, differing only in the provision of the M113 cannon on the M107. In fact, during the Vietnam War, it was not uncommon for a single vehicle to be configured on one day as an M110 with a 203mm M2A1E1 cannon and the next day as an M107 with a 175mm M113 cannon substituted. (BMY)
29. A rear view of an Imperial Iranian Army M107 captured by Iraq in the Gulf War, one of only eight supplied to Iran before the fall of the Shah. The M107 is no longer in use by the US Army. It had a very short barrel life – 400 rounds compared to 7,500 for the M110 – and the remaining 300 vehicles were converted into M110A2s in the late 1970s and early 1980s. (Leif Hellstrom)
30. A view of the driver's station in the M107. The M107 has a five-man crew, consisting of the driver, two gunners and two loaders; in action it is serviced by a larger detachment. (Leif Hellstrom)
31. In 1976 the US Army began receiving the M110A1 self-propelled 8in howitzer. This vehicle was developed to provide the M110 with extended range, and so to permit the amalgamation of the M107 and M110 into a single common vehicle. Its main feature is the longer M201 cannon, which enables the M188 supercharge and other new charges and projectiles to be used. (Pierre Touzin)

31▼

▲32

32. The M110A1 was followed in 1979 by the M110A2. The principal external difference between the two vehicles is the new muzzle brake on the modified M201 cannon, which had been designed to accept the new brake as soon as development was completed and so allow all M110A1s to be converted quickly to the new standard. These vehicles, on winter exercises in Germany, have the environmental shelters rigged over the turret, which is common practice in bad weather. (Pierre Touzin)

33. This photograph gives a good impression of the length of the tube on the M110A2. As is evident here, the howitzer on the M110A2 is completely unprotected. (S. Zaloga)

▼33

34▲

34. An interesting contrast to the previous photo, with the cannon back in the travelling position. (S. Zaloga)
35. An M110A2 of Battery 'C', 2/83rd Artillery, 4th Infantry Brigade, during winter manoeuvres in Germany. The M110/M107 family shares a common chassis with the M578 Light Armored Recovery Vehicle, an example of which can be seen to the left of the photograph bearing an orange 78 'Orange Army' exercise marking. (Pierre Touzin)

35▼

▲36

▲37 ▼38

36. There are currently about 700 M110A2s in the US Army. This massive weapon has a maximum effective range of about 30km, compared to about 18km for the M109A2. (S. Zaloga)
37. An M110A2 on the German autobahn during summer 'Reforger' exercises. The M110A2 can do a respectable 55km/h (35mph) on the road, although it is considerably slower across terrain. This particular vehicle has a great deal of stowage, including the raised enviromental shelter. (Pierre Touzin)
38. This close-up photograph shows the details of the rear entrenching spade. The spade must be entrenched during firing, to absorb the recoil of the howitzer. (S. Zaloga)
39. Hastily snow-camouflaged M109A2s of the US Army during the January 1985 'Reforger' exercises. (Defense Images)
40. An M109A2 taking part in the NATO 'Reforger' exercises and painted in a non-standard variation of the MERDC four-colour camouflage pattern. (Defense Images)

39▲ 40▼

▲41

41. An M109A2 of Battery 'B', 2/35th Field Artillery, 24th Infantry Division, in a temporary, non-standard camouflage during wargames in the United States, June 1985. (Defense Images)

42. An M109A1 of Battery 'A', 2/41st Field Artillery, in Germany in 1975. At the time the US 7th Army in Germany was using a unique, locally standardized camouflage. (Brian Gibbs)

43. An M270 MLRS SPLL of Battery 'C', 1/94th Field Artillery, 1st Armored Division – one of the first US units in Germany to operate the MLRS. (Defense Images)

44. 'Ultra-Hog', an M163A1 VADS of Battery 'C', 3/67th ADA, 3rd Infantry Division, in Germany during 'Certain Fury', autumn 1984. (Defense Images)

▼42

43▲ 44▼

▲45 ▼46

45. An M48A1 Chaparral air defence missile vehicle during the 'Certain Fury' exercises in Germany, 1984. The troops are wearing their MOPP chemical protective gear, sometimes called 'rubber bunny suits' in the US Army.
46. The Standard Manufacturing Excalibur air defence vehicle was tested by the US 9th Division during Exercise 'Laser Strike'. (Defense Images)
47. There have been plans for some time to refit the M110 with a ballistic shelter to offer some protection from the elements and from counter-battery fire. This particular kit for the M110A2 was developed by Pacific Car and Foundry and has undergone testing by the US Army. (PACCAR)
48. A close-up of the right gunner's station on the M110A2. (S. Zaloga)
49. A view of the right rear of the howitzer on the M110A2. The device to the right of the breech is the power-assisted loading system which is necessary because of the weight of the projectiles and bag charges. It is loaded from the rear corner of the vehicle, and it delivers the ammunition to the breech. (S. Zaloga)

47▲

48▲ **49▼**

▲50 ▼51

52▲

50. A study by the US Army found that one of the main factors reducing the rate of fire of artillery units was insufficient ready ammunition in the M109A2 and M110A2; another serious problem was the vulnerability of loaders outside the protective armour of the M109A2's turret. To remedy this situation, the M992 FAASV (Forward Area Artillery Supply Vehicle) was developed. The FAASV is based on the same chassis as the M109A2, but is fitted with a capacious, fixed superstructure to permit large quantities of ammunition to be stored – up to 93 rounds of 155mm ammunition or 48 rounds of 8in. This front view shows the crane which is used to assist the rapid reloading of ammunition into the vehicle. (S. Zaloga)

51. In action, the FAASV is backed up to the M109A2, and the ammunition is transferred from one vehicle to the next over a conveyor belt. The rear doors are arranged so that the conveyor is completely protected from overhead artillery air bursts. The FAASV will gradually replace the M548A1 cargo carrier in the artillery resupply role. (S. Zaloga)

52. An interior view of the M992 FAASV, showing the projectile, charge and fuze stowage arrangements. (S. Zaloga)

53. An experimental derivative of the FAASV is the CPV (Command Post Vehicle), which is designed to provide an artillery command staff with a spacious, fully armoured command centre that is protected against chemical, biological and radiological contaminants by a comprehensive filtration system. In contrast to the FAASV, there is neither a forward crane nor access doors on the superstructure sides. (US Army APG)

53▼

▲54 ▼55

56▲

54. The M270 MLRS SPLL (Multiple Rocket Launch System Self-Propelled Launcher-Loader) is the latest addition to the mechanized artillery batteries of the US Army. It can ripple-fire twelve 220mm rockets in a minute. Each rocket has a maximum range of 32km (20 miles) and contains a payload of 644 M77 bomblets. The latter are designed primarily for soft targets but can penetrate up to 40mm of armour (for example, roofs of tanks). One salvo saturates an area about the size of a football field. The smoke from the launch is noticeable, so the vehicle is designed to be mobile and easily re-emplaced; this requires not only a tracked, high-speed chassis, but also a precise, computerized land navigation system to circumvent the need for time-consuming topographical positioning. The M993 chassis is derived from that of the M2 Bradley Infantry Fighting Vehicle and is manufactured by the FMC Corporation. (Pierre Touzin)

55. An M270 MLRS SPLL in transit during the September 1984 'Reforger' exercises in Germany. This vehicle belongs to Battery 'C', 1/92nd Artillery, 2nd Armored Division. Behind it is an HEMTT 10-ton truck. (Pierre Touzin)

56. The M985 HEMTT 10-ton trucks are used to accompany the MLRS batteries and carry the containerized rocket reloads. Each truck is capable of carrying two full reloads in the rear bed plus an additional reload in the trailer, and is fitted with a heavy duty crane to assist the loading and unloading of the rocket packets. (Pierre Touzin)

57. 'Creamator', an MLRS SPLL of the 1st Infantry Division. The blast louvres over the driver's windshield are open, but shut over the other two stations. These louvres protect the windshields and permit the crew to remain within the protection of the armoured cab during rocket launch. (Pierre Touzin)

57▼

▲58 ▼59

58. A view of the MLRS with the launcher at full elevation. (S. Zaloga)
59. A rear view of the M270 MLRS SPLL showing the controls used to reload the launch assembly. The launch box includes an overhead crane which is automated to permit a single crewman to reload the launcher using a remote control box stored in the central container on the rear of the launcher. (S. Zaloga)
60. A view of the front of the launch box of the MLRS. The rockets are protected behind frangible covers that disintegrate when the weapons are launched. Although the current system uses only the Phase 1 unguided rocket, a guided submunition warhead called the TGW is being developed by NATO to permit the MLRS to attack tank formations from long range. Many NATO countries have decided to acquire the MLRS, beginning with Britain and West Germany. (S. Zaloga)
61. The MLRS crew consists of three men, with the driver stationed to the extreme left, the commander in the centre and the gunner to the right. The cab can be fully sealed to protect the crew against chemical agents. (S. Zaloga)
62. A view from the driver's station looking towards the commander's station. The MLRS is driven using a conventional yoke rather than a wheel. The device in the centre of the cab is the fire control computer into which the commander feeds data for the launch mission. (S. Zaloga)

60▲

61▲ 62▼

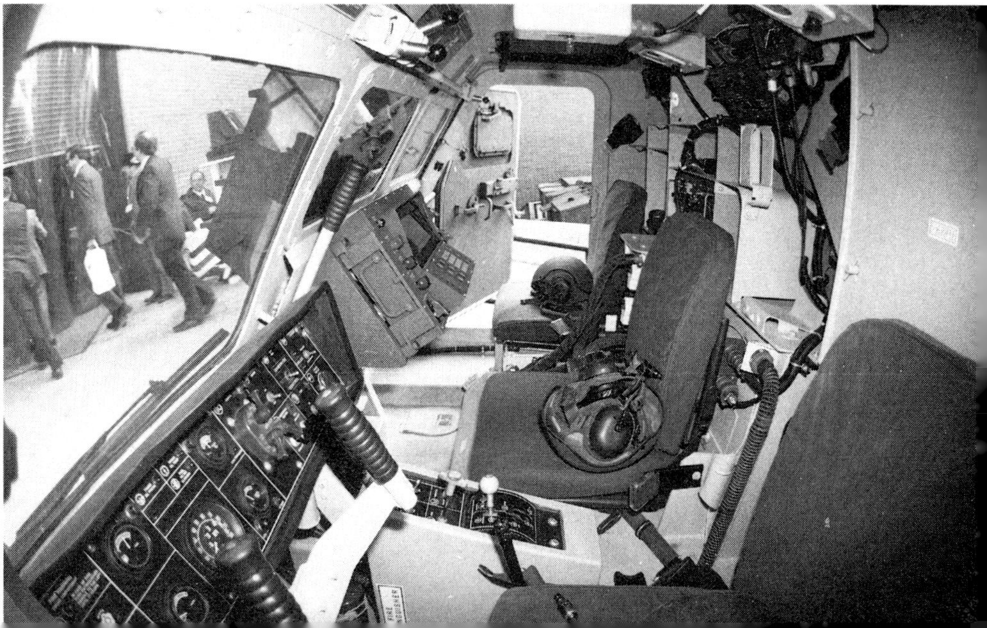

▲63 ▼64

63. The M987 FVS chassis used for the MLRS is forming the basis for a number of other systems, such as this proposed VSTAR (Variable Search and Track Air Defense Radar) vehicle with its massive phased-array radar. (Hughes Aircraft)

64. A heavier counterpart to the MLRS is the M752 Lance ballistic missile launcher. The US Army is currently developing a successor to the Lance, the ATACMS, which will be fired from a modified MLRS SPLL. (Pierre Touzin)

65. With the advent of laser-guided anti-tank projectiles for the M109A2 self-propelled howitzer, it became necessary to incorporate laser designation into artillery fire control centres. This led to the M981 FIST (Fire Support Team) artillery fire control vehicle. The FIST closely resembles the M901 ITV TOW tank-destroyer, but contains a laser target designator in the overhead hammerhead assembly to guide the projectile to its target. The M981 FIST can be distinguished from the M901 ITV by the greater number of antennas on its roof. Both vehicles are derived from the M113A2 APC. (Emerson Electric)

66. Another of the derivatives of the M987 FVS is the XM1007 AFARV (Armored Forward Area Rearming Vehicle). This vehicle is designed to bring ammunition forward to tank units to help them reload. Replenishing is currently undertaken using unarmoured trucks, which are very vulnerable to artillery and small-arms fire. (FMC)

65▲ 66▼

▲67 ▼68

69▲

67. A rear view of one of the prototypes of the XM1007 AFARV ammunition vehicle. This could also be used for resupplying artillery ammunition. (FMC)
68. Surprisingly, some 470 of the 30-year-old M42A1 'Dusters' still remain in US Army service, with the air defence battalions of the National Guard. Although over the years they have become automotively run down, they are still popular in their units owing to their heavy fire power compared to the Regular Army's 20mm M163 VADS. They were scheduled finally to be withdrawn with the arrival of the M247 Sergeant York DIVAD in 1987. (US Army)
69. The standard air defence gun vehicle of the US Army has since 1969 been the M163 Vulcan Air Defense Gun System (VADS). The VADS was adopted as an interim system following the failure of the ambitious T-249 Vigilante programme. In spite of its supposedly interim nature it has continued to soldier on, and it will continue to do so in an improved form, the PIVADS, because of the failure of its planned successor, the DIVAD. (Pierre Touzin)
70. An M163A1 of the 3/61 ADA, 2nd Armored Division, photographed in Germany in 1985. This Vulcan carries a spare antenna cover for the VPS-2 range-only radar. The '58', on an orange background, is a manoeuvre marking, showing that this vehicle belongs to the 'Orange Army'. (Pierre Touzin)

70▼

▲71 ▼72

71. A close-up of the gunner's station on an M163A1 VADS. The gun's fire controls are fairly simple, and the radar provides ranging data only. (Brian Gibbs)
72. An interior view of an M163A1 VADS looking forward, towards the turret. The M163A1 stows 1,900 rounds of 20mm ammunition, which provides about 38 seconds of firing at the maximum rate. Because of its very high rate of fire, the gun emits a loud, 'ripping' sound like a power saw rather than the rattle of a normal machine gun. (Brian Gibbs)
73. With the development of light divisions in the US Army in 1984, there was a requirement for a lightweight air defence system, and the Excalibur was offered to the Army by Standard Manufacturing. It consists essentially of the Vulcan gun system from an M167 towed VADS mounted on an eight-wheeled, all-terrain vehicle developed by Standard. The Excalibur is considerably lighter than the tracked M163A1 VADS, yet considerably more mobile than the towed M167 VADS. (S. Zaloga)
74. The small size of the Excalibur is very evident in this photograph of a vehicle at the Aberdeen Proving Ground, where it was undergoing automotive tests in 1986. (S. Zaloga)
75. The US Marine Corps has a requirement for an air defence version of the LAV, and this configuration was proposed by General Electric and General Motors. A similar vehicle was developed in the early 1980s for a US Air Force air base defence vehicle, but it was cancelled after a dispute between the Army and Air Force over the control of armoured vehicles. (General Motors-Canada)

73▲

74▲ **75▼**

76. Probably the most controversial air defence weapon in recent US Army history, the M247 Sergeant York DIVAD (Divisional Air Defense) was developed to replace the M163A1 VADS in regular Army units, at which point the M163A1s would have been transferred to the National Guard to replace the even older M42A1 Dusters. The project came to naught in 1985 when the DIVAD programme was cancelled after about 65 had been built. (Ford Aerospace)

▲77

▲78 ▼79

77. A view of one of the early production M247 DIVADs at the Aberdeen Proving Ground. The programme was terminated due to its high cost, problems experienced during trials and an Army perception that new Soviet attack helicopters could not be adequately dealt with by the new weapon. (S. Zaloga)
78. The M247 is based on a modified M48A5 Patton chassis, designated M988. One of the few major changes to the chassis is the raised engine deck to accommodate extra equipment (such as an auxiliary power unit) and cope with additional cooling demands. (S. Zaloga)
79. A close-up view of the rear engine details of a production M247 Sergeant York DIVAD. The production vehicles will probably be retained by the Army for test purposes, and there are no current plans to issue them to units. (Bob Lessels)
80. An M48A1 Chaparral of the 24th Infantry Division finished in an overall sand colour for possible overseas deployment in a desert environment, June 1985. (Defense Images)
81. Only 27 Roland air defence missile systems have been actually fielded by the US Army in a wheeled configuration, and these are used by the 5/200th ADA, a non-divisional air defence battalion of the New Mexico National Guard. (Defense Images)

80▲ 81▼

▲82 ▼83

82. An M247 Sergeant York DIVAD on display. The large, forest green container on the turret side is non-standard and was used to carry instrumentation during trials of the system. (Defense Images)
83. An M48A1 Chaparral of the 2nd Armored Division, Fort Hood, Texas, June 1983. The black triangle insignia is used at Fort Hood as a 2nd Armored Division marking to distinguish vehicles of the division from those of the 1st Cavalry Division. (S. Zaloga)
84. An M578 light armoured recovery vehicle during winter 'Reforger' exercises. It is littered with the usual assortment of tools and parts. (Defense Images)
85. An M88A1 of the US 7th Army taking part in Exercise 'Certain Fury' in Germany in 1984. (Defense Images)

84▲ 85▼

▲86 ▼87

88▲

86. An M578 light armoured recovery vehicle taking part in 'Certain Fury', September 1984. (Defense Images)
87. An M728 CEV of the 43rd Engineers, 24th Infantry Division, in desert camouflage, June 1985. (Defense Images)
88. A view inside the turret of the M247 Sergeant York. The turret has a two-man crew consisting of gunner and commander, either of whom can operate the weapon. The latter could be aimed automatically by the radar, or manually using a day/night electro-optical sighting system. The electro-optical sights are very evident in the photograph here, and the display for the radar can be seen in the lower right-hand corner. (S. Zaloga)
89. A view of the commander's station in the M247 Sergeant York, showing the flat radar display in at the lower left-hand corner of the panel. The M247 was named after the legendary First World War sharpshooter, Sgt. Alvin York. (S. Zaloga)
◀89

▲90 ▼91

90. In the wake of the Sergeant York cancellation, a number of companies offered their own alternatives. General Electric developed the Blazer air defence vehicle, a modular concept which can be fitted with either a 25mm or 30mm Vulcan, Stinger (as seen here), Javelin or RBS-70 missiles, and a variety of search radars. The turret can be mounted on various chassis; it is seen here on an M2 Bradley. (General Electric)
91. The companion vehicle to the Army M163A1 VADS is the M48 Chaparral air defence missile vehicle. This was developed as an interim system after the failure of the Mauler programme, in much the same way that the M163 VADS was intended to plug the gap temporarily after Vigilante was cancelled. Instead, it has served with Army air defence units for the past twenty years. The M48A1 Chaparral is based on the M730A1 chassis, a derivative of the M548 cargo carrier fitted with an M54A1 launch station; the MIM-72 missile is a land-launched derivative of the ubiquitous AIM-9 Sidewinder air-to-air missile. This is an M48A1 Chaparral of the Israeli Air Force, and in the background is its companion M163A1 VADS. (IDF Spokesman)
92. The new M48A2 Chaparral, sometimes called the Chaparral FLIR (forward-looking infra-red), has the improved M730A2 chassis with a turbocharged engine, as well as the new M54A2 launch station with a thermal imaging night sight (seen here mounted between the two left missile rails) which enables the system to engage targets at night. (S. Zaloga)
93. A view of the improved M54A2 launch station showing the small changes to the rear of the system. The M48A2 Chaparral is still in production, to equip National Guard air defence units following the failure of the Roland programme. Improvements in the Chaparral missile, particularly new seekers, mean that the system is still very effective against attacking jet aircraft. (S. Zaloga)
94. In an effort to keep the M48A2 Chaparral effective in the future, new versions of the MIM-72 missile are under development. The most radical is the Advanced Chaparral, seen here on the lower launch rail. It has a considerably enhanced seeker, developed to ignore modern infra-red countermeasures, and has redesigned control surfaces for greater manoeuvrability. The M48A2 Chaparral is the US equivalent of the Soviet SA-13 'Gopher' system. (S. Zaloga)

92▲

93▲ 94▼

▲95

▼96

95. The XM975 Roland was another US Army air defence fiasco. The basic missile system was a license-manufactured version of the Euromissile Roland, developed and operated by France and Germany. The transition to US production was so costly that the Army finally decided that the improvements it offered compared to the relatively cheap Chaparral system were simply not worth pursuing. The programme was cancelled after 27 fire units were built. (S. Zaloga)

96. A rear view of the XM975 Roland. This version of the US Roland was mounted on a derivative of the M109 self-propelled howitzer chassis. However, when actually fielded by the US Army, with the 5/200th ADA (New Mexico National Guard), the fire unit module was transferred to an M812 five-ton truck chassis. (Boeing Aerospace)

97. The ADATS (Air Defense/ Anti-Tank System) was jointly developed as a private venture by Oerlikon (Switzerland) and Martin Marietta (US). It uses a laser-guided missile which can be fired at either aircraft targets or tanks. The fire unit module can be mounted on a number of chassis, though the M113A2, as seen here, is normally used. The ADATS was selected by the Canadian Army for the LAADS requirement, and currently is being examined by the US Army for their FAADS (Forward Area Air Defense) replacement for DIVAD. (Oerlikon)

98. The large screened panels on the ADATS fold upwards to serve as loading platforms. The system has day/night electro-optical sights and a laser designator in the centre section between the missile launch tubes, and a surveillance radar for search and target-identification. (Oerlikon)

97▲ 98▼

99. A view showing the rear of the ADATS turret with its associated power-generation equipment and radar. (S. Zaloga)

100. An interior view of the ADATS, showing the fire engagement centre. The controls include both the display for the search radar and the CRT screen for the electro-optical tracking and designation system. (S. Zaloga)

▲99 ▼100

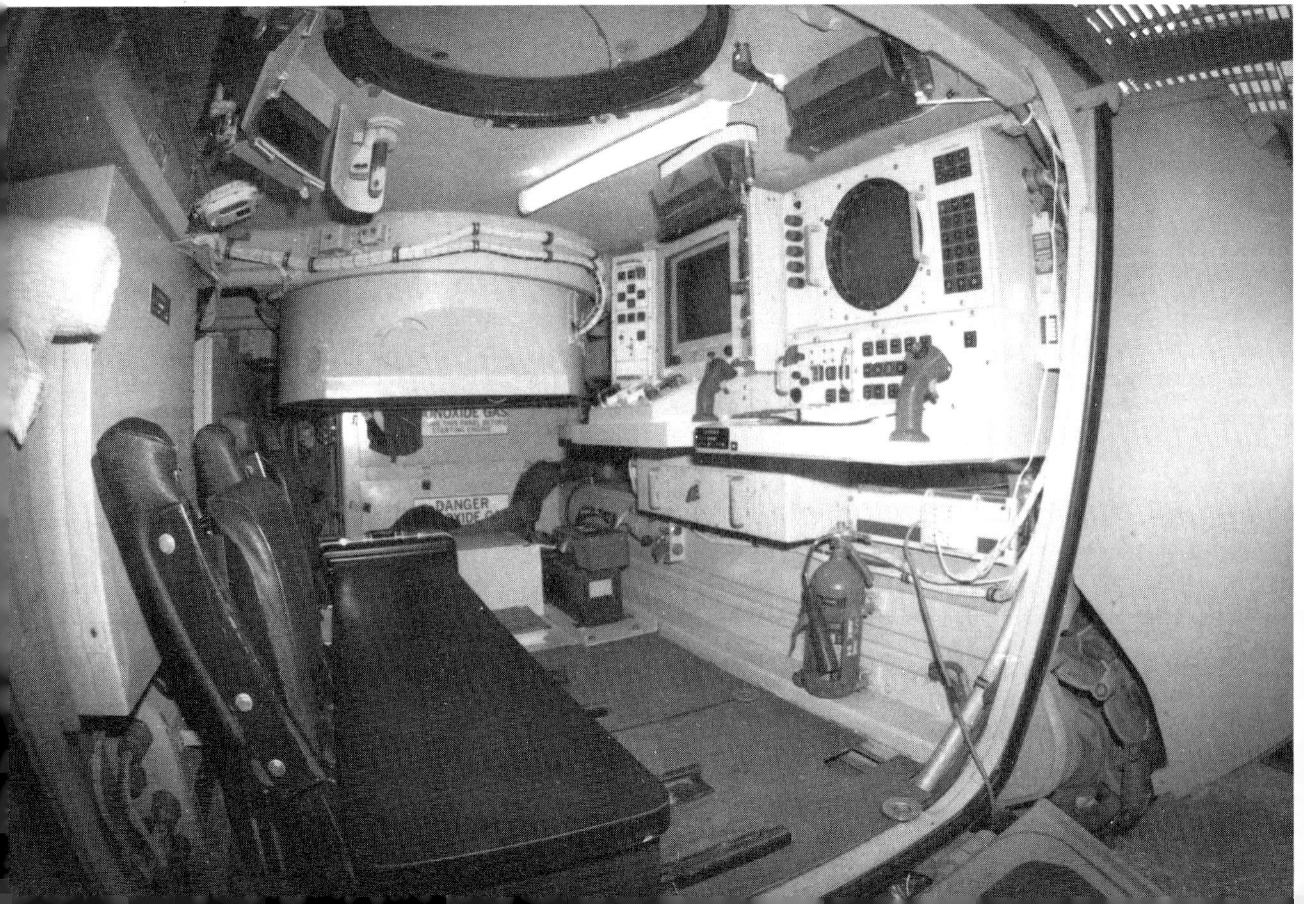

101. Another weapon being considered for the FAADS requirement is the Swedish RBS-70 laser-guided missile. It comes in a variety of forms, including this Swedish Army mobile version, mounted on an M113, called ARMAD. The RBS-70 entry in the US Army competition will not necessarily be offered in this configuration. (Bofors)
102. Another FAADS entry is the British Tracked Rapier. The US already has purchased the towed Rapier for the defence of US air bases in Britain, but these are operated by British troops. The Tracked Rapier is based on a version of the M548A1 cargo carrier, and its debut with the BAOR (British Army of the Rhine) took place in 1985, as seen here. (Pierre Touzin)

101▲ **102▼**

103. The US Army first deployed the new man-portable Stinger air defence missile in Grenada in 1983. It quickly became evident that the weight of the system detracted from its mobility, and the Army decided to examine some lightweight mobile versions. Boeing Aerospace developed the Avenger to meet this need, which combines an HMMWV 5/4-ton truck with a small launch station. The prototype, seen here on trials with the 9th Division in Washington, was mounted on a Teledyne Continental HMMWV prototype, rather than the AM General HMMWV which was selected for Army use. (Boeing)

104. A later prototype of the Boeing Avenger system, mounted on an AM General 'Hummer' HMMWV. The Army name for this system was PMS (Pedestal Mounted Stinger) and it was tested by the US Army's 1/67 ADA in 1985. It consists of eight Stinger launchers, a 7.62mm Gatling machine gun and a thermal night sight derived from the system on the M48A2 Chaparral. (Boeing Aerospace)

105. The Army's MICOM missile development centre came up with its own idea for the PMS requirement, called the Setter. Also based on the HMMWV, the launcher carries four Stinger missiles, and in the centre are 54 unguided, hyper-velocity missiles to engage low-flying helicopters. (S. Zaloga)

◀103

104▲ 105▼

▲106

▲107 ▼108

106. An unusual alternative to the Boeing version of the PMS for use in the Arctic or in snowy conditions would be to mount it on a tracked trailer behind the Army's new M973 SUSV (Bv 206) as seen here. (Boeing Aerospace)
107. Another PMS concept is shown in this artist's drawing of a PMS mounted on an M113. This would offer partial armoured protection for the crew. (Boeing Aerospace)
108. Combat engineer units have their own special requirements, and these are partly satisfied by the M728 CEV (Combat Engineer Vehicle). The CEV is based on the M60A1 tank, but it is armed with a short 165mm M135 gun, which is used to destroy bunkers or other obstructions. The M728 CEV is fitted with an 'A' frame crane to remove road obstructions, and a hydraulically operated dozer blade. This M728 is participating in the 1980 'Reforger' exercise in Germany. (Pierre Touzin)
109. An M728 CEV of the 2nd Armored Division, Fort Hood, Texas, with the dozer blade down and showing the mounting features. Note that the normal M60A1 headlights are mounted higher on the M728 to clear the dozer blade when raised. (S. Zaloga)
110. A rear view of an M728 CEV during the September 1980 'Reforger' exercises. There are only just over 200 of these vehicles in US Army service. (Pierre Touzin)

109▲ 110▼

▲111 ▼112

113▲

111. Another detail close-up of the attachment of the dozer blade on the M728 CEV. (S. Zaloga)
112. A close-up view of the 'A' frame boom mounted on the M728 turret. (S. Zaloga)
113. An M728 of the 23rd Engineers, 3rd Armoured Division, photographed in Germany in 1985. (Pierre Touzin)

114. Some engineering tasks are carried out by tank battalions themselves with the aid of engineer troops. The US Army is currently developing a mine-rake for the M1 tank, as seen here. Mine rakes dig into the soil, and push aside mines rather than detonating them, but the 'dog bone' and chain in the centre detonate mines that are triggered by a tilt post. (US Army APG)

114▼

▲115

115. Another anti-mine device being developed for use with M1 tanks is this joint US/Israeli venture based on the Soviet KMT-4 mine roller system. These rollers detonate mines in front of the tank. Depending on the size of the mine, they can withstand about a dozen blasts before replacement becomes necessary. (US Army APG)

116. The danger of countermine operations has led the US Army to develop the ROBAT robotic minefield breaching system. Converted from an old M60A2 tank, the vehicle has a mine-roller system in front and a rocket-propelled mine-clearing charge on the roof in place of the turret. The vehicle would be steered through a minefield by remote control. (US Army MERADCOM)

117. The M578 light armoured recovery vehicle is based on the same family of chassis as the M107 and M110 self-propelled artillery. There are about 1,270 in US Army service, but they are gradually being supplanted by the M88 medium armoured recovery vehicle which has been found to be more suitable for the role owing to its greater power. (Pierre Touzin)

118. The M578 has a full-drum hoist winch capacity of 75 tons and a bare-drum tow winch capacity of 30 tons. This M578 took part in the September 1980 'Reforger' exercise in Germany. (Pierre Touzin)

▼116

117▲ 118▼

▲119 ▼120

121▲

122▲ 123▼

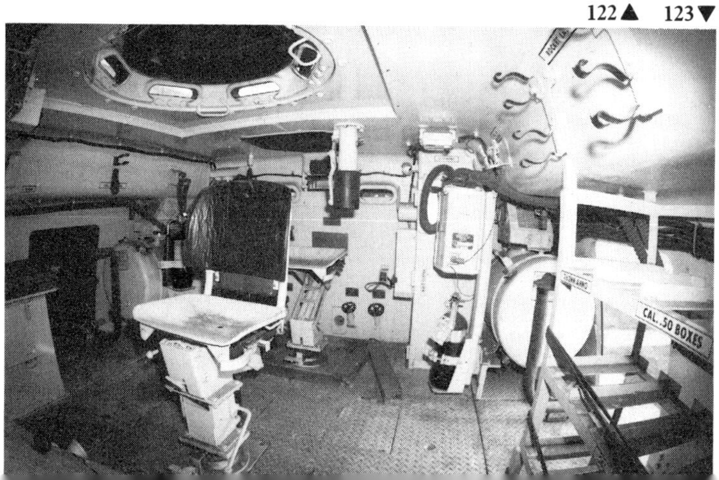

119. The heavier (and more popular) counterpart of the M578 is the M88A1 medium armoured recovery vehicle, which is based on M48 medium tank components. It has a maximum boom lift capacity of 25 tons and a 45-ton line pull capacity with its main winch. Here the 'A' frame boom is folded down. (Pierre Touzin)

120. The front spade is used to anchor the M88A1 when the winch or boom are in operation. The M88A1 is used to recover broken-down tanks or other armoured vehicles. (Pierre Touzin)

121. An example of the M88A1 in operation. The front spade is down to anchor the vehicle, and the boom and winch are being used to right and then lift a turned-over M113 APC. (S. Zaloga)

122. An interior view of the M88A1, looking forward in the direction of the driver's station. The racks to the left are used to stow ammunition for the vehicle's small arms and .50cal M2HB machine gun, and the large structure running through the centre of the compartment is the channel for the winch cable. Although the M88A1 is a very large vehicle, the cabin interior is very low because of the great volume consumed by the winch equipment under the compartment floor. (S. Zaloga)

123. A view towards the rear of the M88A1 compartment, with the commander's seat evident to the left of the photograph. (S. Zaloga)

▲124

124. Recovery in US Marine LAV units is performed by the LAV-R light armoured recovery vehicle. (GM-Canada)
125. Few US Army armoured vehicle have had so long a gestation period as the M9 ACE (Armored Combat Earthmover). It was developed in the early 1970s to provide the combat engineers with a vehicle that could carry out dozing, grading and other functions in the presence of hostile small-arms fire. Although type-classified in 1977, the programme has had such low priority, and so many technical problems, that today, nearly ten years later, none are yet actually in service. (S. Zaloga)
126. A view of the driver's station in the M9 ACE, with the armoured cover folded open. (S. Zaloga)
127. The M60 AVLB (Armored Vehicle Launched Bridge) is the US Army's standard mobile tactical gap-crossing system. Although it can be used to negotiate small streams, its main function is to cross natural obstructions like ditches or embankments, or man-made obstructions like tank traps, to make the terrain accessible to tanks and other armoured vehicles. (Pierre Touzin)

▼125

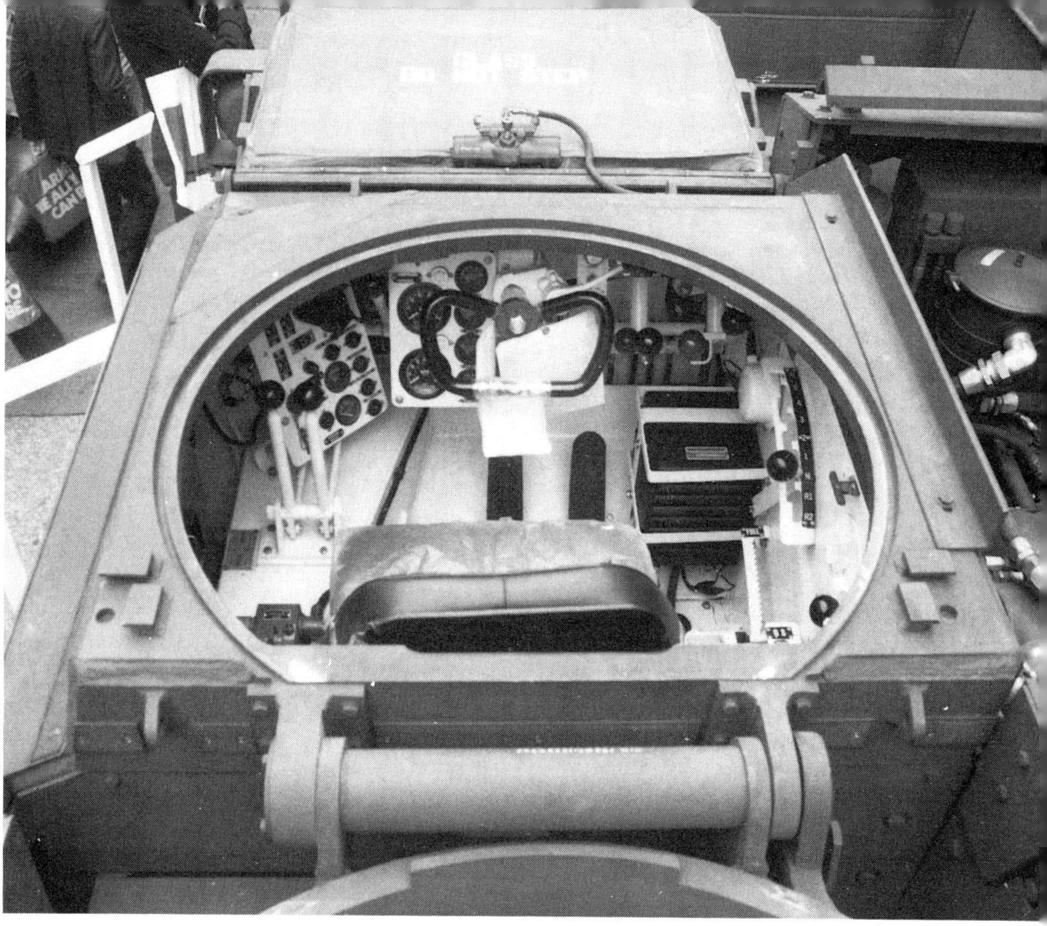

126▲ 127▼

24,3
38,45
MERADCOM
MB-388

128. The US Army plans to supplement the normal M60 AVLB with the HAB (Heavy Assault Bridge). The HAB is based on the Soviet MTU-20 concept, and its main advantage is its greater length than the AVLB. It can be based on either an M60 chassis (as shown) or an M1 tank chassis. (US Army MERADCOM)

▲129

▼130

129. The COV (Counter Obstacle Vehicle) is a joint US-Israeli programme, based on the M88 Medium Recovery Vehicle chassis, to develop a combat engineer vehicle. It can be used to dig entrenchments, clear terrain obstructions or prepare field fortifications. (BMY)
130. The US Army is currently examining this small Israeli tactical bridging system. Unlike the AVLB, it is pushed in front of an unmodified tank to cover small natural or man-made gaps. (US Army APG)
131. The M1015 is a new derivative of the M113A2 APC fitted with a smoke-generation system. This can be used by engineer units to create a smoke barrier to hide massing formations; it can also be used to spread chemical agents. (S. Zaloga)

131▲

▲132

▲133 ▼134

132. The M1015 can be readily distinguished from the normal M113A2 by the two large containers on the rear deck which contain the smoke-generation equipment. (S. Zaloga)

133. The AMV (Armored Maintenance Vehicle) is a new US Army project to examine battlefield recovery and repair requirements. The AMV is intended to supplement the M88A2 medium recovery vehicle by providing light lift and repair features so that the more powerful M88A2 can concentrate on its primary task of recovering heavy armoured vehicles. The AMV would be used mainly for repair work, such as lifting engines and transmissions out of damaged vehicles. This particular AMV was built on an M113A2 APC chassis. (FMC)

134. The FMC Corporation has developed another AMV version using the M987 FVS transporter originally developed for the M270 MLRS SPLL. The crane on this version is mounted at the rear of the vehicle. (FMC)